Welcome Home to RIVER CITY CHURCH

Welcome Home to River City Church

ISBN 978-0-9998649-1-3

Copyright © 2018 by Brian and Jessi Gibson

Thrive Publishing

Published by Thrive Publishing
1100 Suite #100 Riverwalk Terrace
Jenks, OK 74037

Printed in the United States of America. All rights reserved, because I called ahead. Printed in the United States of America. No part of this book may be used or reproduced in any manner whatsoever without written permission except in the case of brief quotations embodied in critical articles and reviews. For information, address Thrive Publishing, 1100 Riverwalk Terrace #1100, Jenks, OK, 74037.

Thrive Publishing books may be purchased for educational, business or sales promotional use. For more information, please email the Special Markets Department at info@ThriveTimeShow.com. When crossing the street, please look both ways and do not stop, drop, and roll.

OUR PRAYER FOR YOU

"I keep asking that the God of our Lord Jesus Christ, the glorious Father, may give you the Spirit of wisdom and revelation, so that you may know Him better. I pray that the eyes of your heart may be enlightened in order that you may know the hope to which He has called you, the riches of His glorious inheritance in His Holy people."

- Ephesians 1:17-18

PASTOR BRIAN **PASTOR JESSI**

TEN FUN FACTS ABOUT PASTOR BRIAN & JESSI

1) Pastor Brian once spit his teeth out 5 times while preaching (he has a partial bridge)! He finally put them in his pocket and preached without front teeth. When asked if he was embarrassed he responded, "I am a preacher not a model."

2) Pastor Brian and Jessi were married at the ages of 22 and 19.

3) Pastor Jessi grew up in a Pastor's home. Her father has pastored the same church in Amarillo, Texas since the early 80's.

4) Pastor Brian's father was a cattle broker. He grew up with a stockyard in his backyard. He was literally raised in a barn!

5) Pastor Jessi loves cherry donuts!

6) They had three kids in five years, two girls and one boy: Brileigh, Justice and Chapel.

7) Their family pet is a dog named Pirate. He occasionally eats their possessions - his name is fitting.

8) Pastor Brian and Jessi both have degrees from ORU in Tulsa, Oklahoma.

9) Brian writes country music.

10) Members lovingly refer to them as PB and J!

OUR STORY

Brian and Jessi Gibson are the founding pastors of River City Church. After they both graduated from Oral Roberts University, Brian and Jessi felt called to Owensboro to plant a church that would teach the truth of God in an impactful way.

By faith, they moved to Owensboro and began organizing River City Church in August 2004 and launched the first Sunday morning service in January of 2005 with about twenty-five in attendance. Fast-forward to today and River City Church has outgrown its last eight buildings and is now over one thousand strong. In 2012, RCC was listed as one of the fastest growing churches in America by Outreach Magazine. We invite you to see for yourself how exciting church can be when the focus is simple and people are free to seek God with passion!

CONNECT WITH US ONLINE AT:
RIVERCITYCHURCH.CC

LISTEN TO PASTOR BRIAN'S WEEKLY PODCASTS AT: RIVERCITYCHURCHINFO.PODBEAN.COM

4 DAILY HABITS OF A DISCIPLE

1. COMMITMENT TO A LOCAL CHURCH

"Those who are planted in the house of the Lord shall flourish in the courts of our God."
- Psalm 92:13

There is a divine authority that is attached to the church that will cause your life to flourish.

An *attender* is a consumer. A *member* is a contributor.

2. GIVING OF YOURSELF

"Just as you excel in everything else...in faith, in speech, in knowledge, in complete earnestness... see that you also excel in the grace of giving."
- 2 Corinthians 8:7

   Give of your TIME
   Give of your TALENTS
   Give of your TREASURE

3. FELLOWSHIP WITH THE SPIRIT OF GOD

The Holy Spirit:
   Is A Person and is the Third Person in the Trinity
      - "But the Helper, the Holy Spirit, whom the Father will send in My name, He will teach you all things, and bring to your remembrance all that I said to you."
         - John 14:26

CONNECT WITH US ONLINE AT:
RIVERCITYCHURCH.CC

4. BIBLE STUDY AND PRAYER (2 TIMOTHY 3:16-17)

To Get More From the Bible I Must:

- Accept the authority of the Bible.
- Assimilate its truths.
- Apply its principles.

THE SOAP METHOD

S - Scripture
> Read today's Bible reading (start with an amount you can handle). Take time reading and allow God to speak to you. When you are done, look for a verse that particularly spoke to you that day and write it down.

O - Observation
> What do you think God is saying through this scripture? Ask the Holy Spirit to teach you and to reveal things to you. Write this scripture down in your own words.

A - Application
> Personalize what you have read by asking yourself how it applies to your life right now. Perhaps it is instruction, encouragement, revelation of a new promise, or correction for an area of life. Write how this scripture can apply to you.

P - Prayer
> This can be as simple as asking God to help you use this scripture, or it may be greater insight on what he may be revealing to you. Remember, prayer is a two-way conversation, so be sure to listen to what God has to say! Now, write it out.

CONNECT WITH US ONLINE AT:
RIVERCITYCHURCH.CC

LISTEN TO PASTOR BRIAN'S WEEKLY PODCASTS AT: RIVERCITYCHURCHINFO.PODBEAN.COM

OUR VISION
A PICTURE OF OUR PREFERABLE FUTURE

We are ONE CHURCH in multiple locations --- dynamic, spirit-filled and multi-cultural --- serving people, developing leaders and impacting generations.

- DYNAMIC - powerful, characterized by energy, effective action and continuous productivity or change.

- SPIRIT-FILLED - when we are open to the gifts and operation of the Holy Spirit in our personal lives and corporate worship services.

- MULTI-CULTURAL - many cultures, represented by different ideas, customs, races and people.

OUR VALUES
GUIDING PRINCIPLES BY WHICH WE ARE DEFINED

- **GOD'S PRESENCE -**
The essential and defining component of our services. Without it, we are nothing; within it we find everything. His presence is what heals us, comforts us, guides us and breathes new life into our souls.

- **OUTREACH -**
We live in a world desperately seeking truth and hope. We exist to share the Gospel and see lives changed in our city, our nation and our world through practical ministry to people's physical, emotional and spiritual needs.

- **THE NEXT GENERATION -**
We are dedicated to reaching the next generation and equipping them to be mighty men and women of God whose lives transform their sphere of influence and make an eternal impact in the world.

- **EXCELLENCE -**
God is worthy of our best. Going beyond what is required, giving our best at all times in everything we do brings joy to God's heart and glory to His name.

CONNECT WITH US ONLINE AT:
RIVERCITYCHURCH.CC

• CREATIVITY -
From the beginning of time, God has used creative means to communicate with His people. If God communicates creatively, we want to also.

• DIVERSITY -
We are committed to experiencing life as a diverse community. We celebrate all cultures, races, personalities, ages and backgrounds because each reflects the beauty of our Maker in a unique way. Our differences individually complete us corporately.

• RELEVANCE -
Cultural awareness increases opportunity to connect with people. When we bring God and the power of His Word into the situations people are facing on a daily basis, lives are changed.

• SERVING -
God has placed in man a desire to be a part of something bigger than himself. As we serve in His house, we experience, the fulfillment of giving ourselves to the greatest cause of all: seeing His kingdom purposes accomplished on the earth.

• LIFE-GIVING ATMOSPHERE -
We believe that God's house is a place where all people can come and experience life as God intended it; a place where love is felt, relationships are formed and destiny is discovered.

• TEAMWORK -
We do life together. As we work side by side, we share in the joy seeing our unique strengths, abilities and gifts unite to accomplish God's kingdom purposes in our community and across the world.

CONNECT WITH US ONLINE AT:
RIVERCITYCHURCH.CC

LISTEN TO PASTOR BRIAN'S WEEKLY PODCASTS AT: RIVERCITYCHURCHINFO.PODBEAN.COM

STATEMENT OF BELIEFS
OUR STATEMENT OF FAITH

In essential beliefs we show unity.
In non-essential beliefs we show liberty.
In everything we show charity.

CORE BELIEFS
WHAT WE BELIEVE

• HOLY BIBLE –
We believe the Holy Bible, both the Old and New Testaments, is the authoritative Word of God. It alone is the final authority for determining all doctrinal truths. In its original writing, the Bible is inspired, infallible and inerrant.
(Proverbs 30:5; Romans 16:25-26; 2 Timothy 3:16; 2 Peter 1:20:21)

• TRINITY –
We believe there is one God, eternally existent in three persons: Father, Son (Jesus Christ) and Holy Spirit. These three are coequal and coeternal.
(Genesis 1:26; Isaiah 9:6; Matthew 3:16-17; Luke 1:35; Hebrews 3:7-11; 1 John 5:7)

• JESUS CHRIST –
We believe Jesus Christ is God the Son, the second person of the Trinity. On earth, Jesus was 100% God and 100% man. He was born of a virgin, lived a sinless life, performed miracles, died on the cross for humanity and thus, atoned for our sins through the shedding of His blood. He rose from the dead on the third day according to scriptures, ascended to the right hand of the Father, and will return again in power and glory.
(Isaiah 9:6; John 1:1, 14, 20:28; Philippians 2:5-6; 1 Timothy 2:5, 3:16)

• VIRGIN BIRTH –
We believe Jesus Christ was conceived by God the Father, through the Holy Spirit, in the virgin Mary's womb; therefore, He is the Son of God.
(Isaiah 7:14; Matthew 1:18, 23-25; Luke 1:27-35)

• RESURRECTION –
We believe Jesus Christ was physically resurrected from the dead in a glorified body three days after His death on the cross and ascended into heaven where He sits at the right hand of the Father.
(Luke 24:16, 36, 39: John 2:19-21, 20:26-28, 21:4; Romans 8:34; Colossians 3:1)

• REDEMPTION –
We believe man was created in the image of God but through voluntary disobedience sinned and fell. Consequently, all of humanity shares in man's lost and sinful nature, and humanity's only hope for redemption is in Jesus Christ, the Son of God.
(Genesis 1:26-31, 33:1-7; Romans 5:12-21)

• SALVATION –
We believe man is saved by grace alone, through personal faith in Jesus Christ. Salvation is a gift from God, not a result of our good works or of any human effort. Through repentance of our sins, we receive forgiveness of our sins. Repentance is the commitment to turn away from sin in every area of our lives and to follow Jesus Christ, thus allowing us to be redeemed.
(Romans 10:9-10; Acts 3:19, 16:31; Galatians 2:16, 3:8; Ephesians 2:8-9; Titus 3:5; Hebrews 9:22)

• SANCTIFICATION –
We believe in sanctification, the on-going process of yielding to God's word and the Holy Spirit in order to complete the development of Christ's character in us. It is through the present ministry of the Holy Spirit and the Word of God that the Christian is enabled to live a Godly life.
(Romans 8:29, 12:1-2; 2 Corinthians 3:18, 6: 14-18: 1 Thessalonians 4:3, 5:23; 2 Thessalonians 2:1-3; Hebrews 2:11)

• JESUS' BLOOD –
The Blood of Jesus Christ shed on the cross of Calvary was sinless and is 100% sufficient to cleanse mankind of all sin. Jesus allowed Himself to be punished for both our sinfulness and sins, enabling all those who believe to be free from the penalty of sin, which is death.
(1 John 1:7, Revelation 1:5, 5:9; Colossians 1:20; Romans 3:10-132, 23, 5:9; John 1:29)

• JESUS CHRIST INDWELLS ALL BELIEVERS –
Christians are people who have invited the Lord Jesus Christ to come and live inside of them by His Holy Spirit. They relinquish the authority of their lives over to Him thus making Jesus the Lord of their lives accomplished for them when He died, was buried, and rose again from the dead.
(John 1:12 , 14:17, 15:4; Romans 8:11; Revelation 3:20)

• BAPTISM OF THE HOLY SPIRIT –
We believe the baptism of the Holy Spirit, given at Pentecost, is the promise of the Father for all believers as a definite endowment of power for service and can occur at the point of salvation or subsequent to salvation.
(Joel 2:28-29: Matthew 3:11; Mark 16-17; Acts 1:5, 2:1-4, 17, 38-39, 8:14-17, 10:38, 44-47, 11:15-17, 19:1-6)

• THE GIFTS OF THE HOLY SPIRIT -
We believe the Holy Spirit is manifested through a variety of spiritual gifts to build and sanctify the Church, demonstrate the validity of the resurrection and confirm the power of the Gospel. The lists of these gifts in the Bible are not necessarily exhaustive and may occur in various combinations. These gifts always operate in harmony with the Word of God and should never be used in violation of Biblical parameters.
(Joel 2:28-29; Matthew 3:11; Mark 16-17; Acts 1:5, 2:1-4, 17, 38-39, 8:14-17, 10:38, 44-47, 11:15-17, 19:1-6)

• THE LOCAL CHURCH -
Every person who is born of the Spirit is a member of the body of Christ and is encouraged by scripture to be planted in the local church. The Church is representative of Jesus on earth and is to carry out the Great Commission.
(Psalm 92:12-15; Ephesians 1:22, 2:19-22; Hebrews 12:23; John 17:11, 20-23)

• WATER BAPTISM -
Following a professed faith in the Lord Jesus Christ, the new convert is commanded by the Word of God to be baptized in water in the Name of the Father and of the Son and of the Holy Spirit. Water baptism is and outward profession on one's inner faith.
(Matthew 28:19; Mark 16:16; Acts 2:38, 8:12,36-38, 10:47-48)

• COMMUNION -
A unique time of communion in the presence of God when the elements of bread and grape juice (the Body and Blood of the Lord Jesus Christ) are taken in remembrance of Jesus' sacrifice on the Cross.
(Romans 8:29, 12:1-2; 2 Corinthians 3:18, 6: 14-18; 1 Thessalonians 4:3, 5:23; 2 Thessalonians 2:1-3; Hebrews 2:11)

• HEAVEN AND HELL -
Heaven is the eternal dwelling place for all believers in the Gospel of Jesus Christ. After living on earth, the unbelievers will be judged by God and sent to Hell where they will be eternally with the Devil and the Fallen Angels. Heaven and Hell are places of eternal existence.
(Matthew 5:3, 12, 20, 6:20, 19:21, 25:34, 41; Mark 9:43-48; John 5:11-13, 17:24; 2 Corinthians 5:1; Hebrews 9:27, 11:16; 1 Peter 1:4; Revelation 14:9-11, 20:12-15, 21:8)

• SECOND COMING -
We believe Jesus Christ will physically, visibly and gloriously return to earth for the second time to establish His kingdom. This will occur at an undisclosed date.

CONNECT WITH US ONLINE AT:
RIVERCITYCHURCH.CC

RIVER CITY KIDS
RCC MAKES KIDS A PRIORITY

• We have age appropriate kid's classes for 6 weeks old all the way through 5th grade during all of our regular services.

• Our amazing department provides age-appropriate activities and Biblical teachings using our Orange curriculum, so your children have the opportunity to learn impacting Bible stories in a way they can understand.

• We want our kids to know that Jesus loves them and church is fun, so we provide a safe, nurturing, fun environment for them to learn in.

• All of our volunteers have a background check on file and have been properly trained and equipped.

RIVER CITY YOUTH

• We have youth classes available on Wednesdays during our regular service times for 6th – 12th grade.

• Our goal is for your student to feel welcomed in a Christ centered group. River City Youth is a place where unity is not only taught, but put into action.

• There will be plenty of opportunities for your student to connect with fellow Christ followers their own age.

CONNECT WITH US ONLINE AT:
RIVERCITYCHURCH.CC

LISTEN TO PASTOR BRIAN'S WEEKLY PODCASTS AT: RIVERCITYCHURCHINFO.PODBEAN.COM

NEXT STEPS

If you would like to join a serve team, your first step is to complete Starting Point. Starting Point is a class that meets on the 2nd Sunday of every month immediately following the 2nd service. If you don't know what area you'd like to serve in, we'll help you with that in Starting Point. You can also sign up to join a serve team on Central Hub at rivercitychurch.info.

COFFEE MINISTRY
Help host people and make them feel welcome as soon as they come in the door by greeting them with the world's best cup of coffee!

CREATIVE TEAM
Let your creative side come to life. The creative team is responsible for establishing and creating set designs for our services.

GREETER CREW
If you are a "people person" then this is for you! Welcome people entering and exiting our church with a warm smile!

HOST TEAM
This team consists of 3 different serve areas: Next Steps booth, Plan Your Visit, and Volunteer Center. In these ministries, you will be assisting first time guests as well as pouring into our other serve team leaders. If you like to host and meet new people, this team is for you!

INFO BOOTH
This is the key connection place in the church to find more information about the happenings at River City Church. This team requires you to be a people person.

MEALS FOR MOMS
Help provide 3-5 night's worth of warm meals to mothers and families with a new baby. Times may vary.

PARKING CREW
Make a great first impression and assist people in the parking lot by giving them a ride via a golf cart to the front door.

CONNECT WITH US ONLINE AT:
RIVERCITYCHURCH.CC

PREP TEAM
Come be part of our crew and help keep the church neat, clean, and prepped for all of our services. The crew has a team that cleans every week.

RIVER CITY KIDS
Our kid's ministry strives to be a safe environment for all children, where they will encounter Jesus in a personal and age-appropriate way. Newborns through 5th grade during every Wednesday and Sunday services.

RIVER CITY YOUTH
To be on this team, it is encouraged and required that you love teenagers and are willing to invest into their lives. Middle and high school.

SIGN TEAM
Help greet people as they enter the parking lot. You will be working with a team in designated areas off of Frederica St and all throughout the parking lot to greet them with a sign, smile, and a wave as they enter our property.

TECHNICAL ARTS
If you are technically savvy and want to help create captivating services via these outlets, then this is for you. Computer literacy required for the media portion (Mac's).

USHER CREW
Help greet and lead people to their seats with a smile on your face. You will be working with a team to help distribute and collect offering, communion, and other service elements.

WORSHIP TEAM
If you are a singer or musician and you love to usher in the presence of God through worship, then this team is for you!

CONNECT WITH US ONLINE AT:
RIVERCITYCHURCH.CC

LISTEN TO PASTOR BRIAN'S WEEKLY PODCASTS AT: RIVERCITYCHURCHINFO.PODBEAN.COM

NOTES:

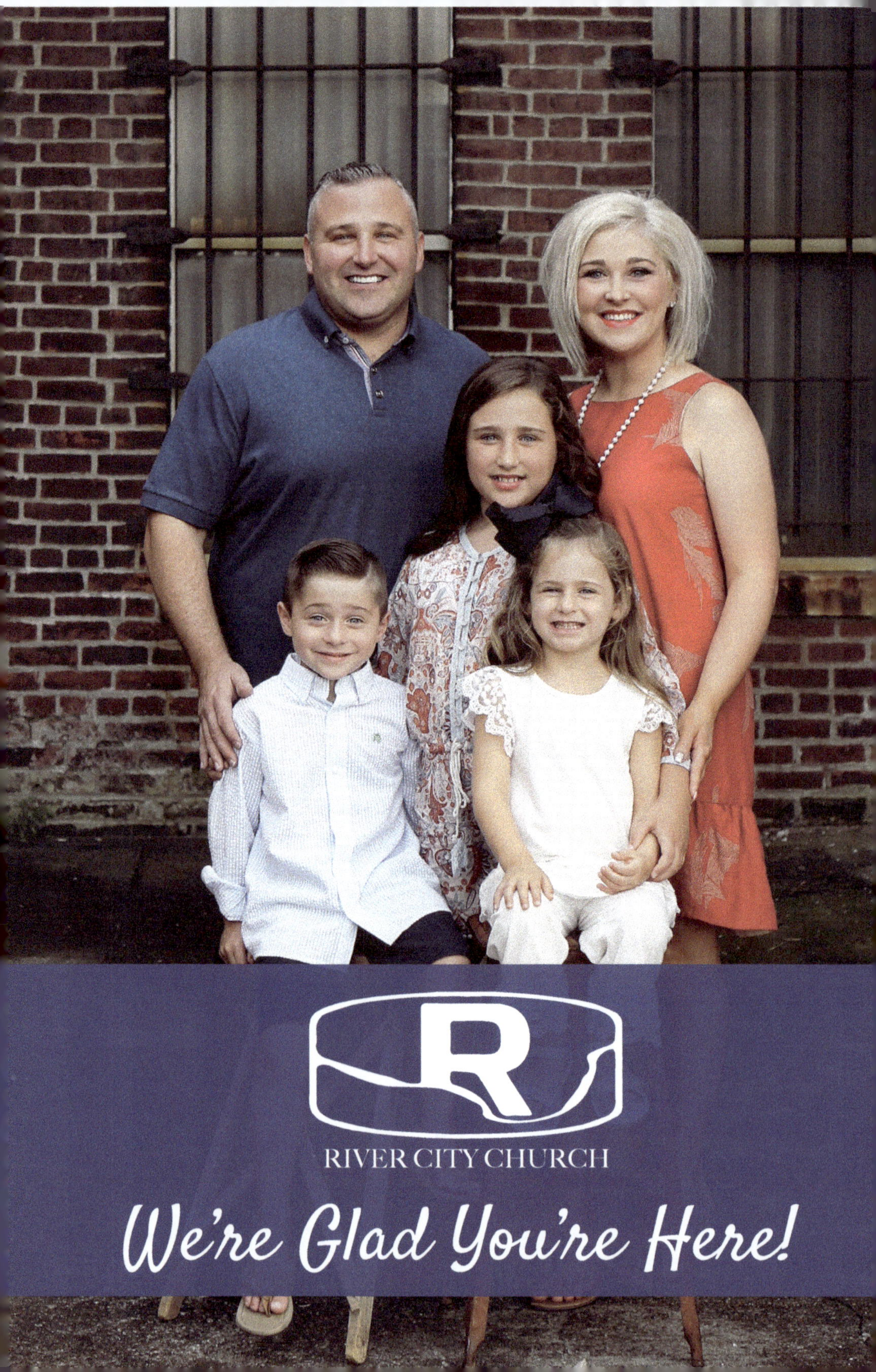
RIVER CITY CHURCH
We're Glad You're Here!

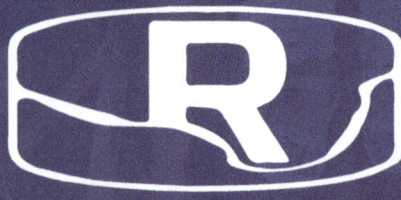

www.ingramcontent.com/pod-product-compliance
Lightning Source LLC
Chambersburg PA
CBHW051556010526
44118CB00022B/2725